Heavenly Manna

The Southern Desserts Collection

Created & Compiled by:

Peggy Donegan Snipes

The house of Israel named it manna, and it was like coriander seed, white and its taste was like wafers with honey.   Exodus 16:31

Good things come
to those who bake.

PEACH PIE

2 uncooked pie shells
2 large can peach pie filling
¼ cup ground nutmeg
1/8 teaspoon salt
2 teaspoons lemon juice
1/8 teaspoon almond extract
Mix all ingredients.

Pour mixture into unbaked pie shell.
Place second pie shell over the top, cut slices into crust to vent.

Bake at 375 degrees for 50 to 60 minutes.

Dot with butter.
Sprinkle with sugar.

For homemade pie crust see page 69.

APPLE PIE

2 uncooked pie shells
2 large can apple pie filling
¼ cup sugar
¼ cup brown sugar
1 teaspoon cinnamon
¼ teaspoon ground nutmeg
Mix all ingredients together.

Pour into unbaked pie shell.
Place second pie shell across the top and cut slices into shell to vent.

Bake at 375 degrees for 50 to 60 minutes.

Dot with butter.
Sprinkle with sugar.

For homemade pie crust see page 69.

CHERRY PIE

2 uncooked pie shells
2 large cans cherry pie filling
1 cup sugar
¼ teaspoon almond extract
¼ teaspoon salt

Mix ingredients and pour into pie shell.

Cover with second pie shell and cut to vent OR using a pizza cutter, cut pie crust into strips and create lattice across pie.

Bake at 375 degrees for 50 to 60 minutes.
Dot top with butter.
Sprinkle with sugar.

For homemade pie shell see page 69.

RUM CAKE

CAKE INGREDIENTS:

1 box of yellow cake mix
4 beaten eggs
½ cup water
½ cup chopped pecans
1 box vanilla pudding
½ cup canola oil
½ cup cooking rum
1 tbsp. vanilla

Grease Bundt pan and sprinkle pecans in the bottom. Mix all the above ingredients together and pour into pan. Bake at 350 degrees for about 1 hour or until done.

ICING INGREDIENTS:

1 cup sugar
¼ cup cooking rum
¼ cup water

Boil together for 2 minutes and add ¾ stick of butter. Continue to stir until melted. Pour hot mixture over hot cake while still in pan. Cool.

LEMON BLUEBERRY BREAD

Bread:

1 cup sugar
1/3 cup melted butter
1 tsp. baking powder
3 tbsp. lemon juice
1 ½ cups flour
½ tsp. salt
1 cup blueberries
2 tbsp. lemon peel
½ cup crushed nuts – optional
2 eggs
½ cup milk
Bake at 350 degrees for 1 hour or until a toothpick can be inserted and then removed clean.

Glaze:

2 tbsp. lemon juice
¼ cup sugar
Mix together and pour over hot bread.

PUMPKIN PIE

1 ½ cup granulated sugar
1 tsp. salt
2 tsp. ground cinnamon
1 tsp. ground ginger
½ tsp. ground cloves
4 large eggs
1 20oz. can pumpkin
2 12 oz. cans evaporated milk
2 unbaked 9" deep-dish pie shells

Mix sugar, salt, cinnamon, ginger and cloves in small bowl.
Beat eggs in large bowl.
Stir in pumpkin and sugar-spice mixture.
Gradually stir in evaporated milk.
Pour into pie shells.
Preheat oven to 425 degrees. Reduce temperature to 350 and bake for 40 to 50 minutes or until toothpick inserted in middle comes out clean.
Cool.

PEANUT BUTTER FUDGE

3 cups white vanilla baking chips
1 can sweetened condensed milk
½ cup smooth or nutty peanut butter

Line an 8" pan with foil and spray with cooking spray.

Add all ingredients in a microwave safe bowl and cook at 1-minute increments (stirring between) until smooth.

Immediately spread into pan and let stand for 2 hours to set before cutting.

Keep refrigerated and use within 5 days.

SUN DROP CAKE

2 sticks melted butter
½ cup shortening
3 cups sugar
5 beaten eggs
1 tbsp. vanilla
1 tbsp. lemon flavoring
3 cups sifted flour
¾ cup Sun Drop orange

Cream butter and shortening. Add in sugar gradually.
Add flavoring, flour and Sun Drop.
Pour into large greased pan.
Bake at 325 degrees for 1 hour and 15 minutes or until
tooth pick can be inserted in middle and removed clean.

Glaze:

2 tbsp. melted butter
2 cups confectioner's sugar
2 tablespoons Sun Drop

Mix together and spread over hot cake. Cool.

CHOCOLATE CHIP COOKIES

2 ¼ cups flour
1 tsp. baking powder
1 tsp. sea salt
2 sticks melted butter (1 cup)
¾ cup sugar
¾ cup packed brown sugar
1 tsp. vanilla
2 large eggs
2 cups chocolate chip morsels
1 cup chopped nuts (your preference)

Preheat oven to 375 degrees.
Mix all ingredients together.
Refrigerate for 5 to 10 minutes.
Use spoon to scoop out and round into balls or drops.
Place on baking sheet.
Bake for 9 to 12 minutes.
Remove from sheet and let cool.

SNICKERDOODLE BARS

1 16.5oz roll of sugar cookies OR
  from scratch on page 79
1 ¼ tsp. cinnamon
1 tsp. sugar
1 16oz vanilla ready to spread frosting

Preheat oven to 350 degrees.

Mix cookie dough and 1 tsp. of cinnamon.
Press evenly into greased 8" pan.
Bake 25 minutes or until edges are brown. Cool for approximately 1 hour.

Spread frosting across bars.
Stir remaining cinnamon and sugar until blended then sprinkle across top of frosting.

COCONUT PECAN CHOCOLATE FUDGE

1 cup milk chocolate chips
1 can chocolate frosting
2 tsp. vanilla
2 cups chopped pecans
2 cups sweetened shredded toasted coconut
1 cup vanilla baking chips
1 can coconut pecan frosting

Line 9" pan with foil and cover with cooking spray.
Microwave chocolate chips in 1 minute intervals (stirring between) until smooth and melted.
Stir in chocolate frosting and 1 tsp. of vanilla.
Stir in ½ of the nuts and ½ of the coconut.
Spread into pan.
Microwave vanilla chips in 1 minute intervals (stirring between) until smooth and melted.
Stir in coconut pecan frosting and 1 tsp. vanilla.
Stir in the remaining nuts and coconut.
Spread over chocolate mixture and sprinkle nuts.
Refrigerate 1 ½ hours until firm. Store covered in refrigerator.

PRALINE CANDIES

1 ½ cups firmly packed light brown sugar
½ cup heavy whipping cream
1 tbsp. light corn syrup
¼ tsp. salt
2 tbsp. unsalted butter
1 cup chopped pecans
½ tsp. vanilla

Line cookie sheet with wax paper or use cooking spray.
In pan bring the brown sugar, corn syrup, salt, and cream
to a boil over medium heat. Stir until sugar dissolves and
reaches 236 degrees on a candy thermometer.
Remove from heat and place the butter in the center of
the mixture. Do not stir.
When mixture reaches 150 degrees, use a wooden spoon
and stir in pecans and vanilla.
Stir continuously until candy begins to thicken. 4-5
minutes.
Drop mixture by tablespoons onto the prepared pan.
Let stand until firm.
Store up to 1 week in air tight container.

DING – A – LINGS

1 large can (3 ½ cups) of chow Mein noodles
2 cups mini marshmallows
1 11oz butter scotches
½ cup peanut butter

In pan melt butter scotches and peanut butter over medium heat until smooth.

Remove from heat.

Stir in marshmallows and noodles.

Quickly spoon onto parchment paper.

Let set.

CHOCOLATE BUTTER CAKE

1 box devil's food cake mix
¾ cup melted butter
3 eggs
1 8oz package softened cream cheese
2 tbsp. unsweetened baking cocoa
2 cups powdered sugar
2 tsp. vanilla
1 cup semisweet chocolate chips
Whip cream

Preheat oven to 350 degrees. Grease 13x9 baking dish.
Mix cake mix, ½ cup of the melted butter, 1 egg and 1 tsp. of vanilla. Press in bottom of baking dish and set to the side.
Mix cream cheese until smooth.
Add 2 eggs and cocoa and mix until smooth.
On low, add powdered sugar then ¼ cup of melted butter and 1 tsp. of vanilla.
Stir in chocolate chips.
Spread in pan over cake mixture.
Bake for 45 minutes or until tooth pick can be inserted in the middle and removed clean.
Serve topped with whipped cream.

LEMON LOAF

1 box white cake mix
2 6oz lemon burst yogurt cups
½ cup melted butter
1 tbsp. grated lemon peel
2 eggs
2 tsp. sugar

Heat oven to 350 degrees. Grease or line a 9x5 pan.

Mix cake mix, yogurt, butter, lemon peel and eggs on low until mixed. Move to medium speed for 2 minutes. Pour batter into pan. Sprinkle with course sugar.

Bake 40 to 50 minutes or until toothpick inserted into middle can be removed clean. Cool completely.

LEMON CHEESECAKE BARS

1 box yellow cake mix
¼ softened butter
3 eggs
1 8oz. softened cream cheese
1 cup powdered sugar
2 tsp. grated lemon peel
2 tbsp. lemon juice

Heat oven to 350 degrees. Ungreased 13x9 pan.

Mix dry cake mix, butter and 1 egg on low until crumbly.

Beat cream cheese on medium until smooth. Beat in powdered sugar on low.
Stir in lemon peel and lemon juice until smooth. Reserve ½ cup in refrigerator.

Beat remaining 2 eggs into cream cheese mixture on medium until smooth. Spread over cake mixture.

Bake 25 minutes or until set. Cool.

Spread reserved cream cheese over mixture. Refrigerate until firm. Store covered in refrigerator.

WALNUT BANANA BREAD

¾ cup sugar
1 ½ cups flour
½ tsp. baking soda
½ tsp. salt
¼ tsp. cinnamon
2 eggs
½ tsp. vanilla
2 very ripe bananas mashed well
1 cup walnuts (or substitute chocolate chips)

Mix all ingredients together until smooth.
Pour into lined or greased pan.
Bake at 300 degrees for 45 minutes or until a toothpick
can be inserted and then removed clean.

STRAWBERRY CA

Cake:

1 box strawberry cake mix
1 box strawberry jello
½ cup water
4 eggs

Mix ingredients until blended and then add:

¾ cup oil
¾ cup strawberries

Mix well and pour into a greased or lined pan.
Bake at 350 degrees for 30 to 40 minutes or until a
toothpick can be inserted and then removed clean.

Icing:

1 cup sifted powdered sugar
¼ cup melted butter
¾ cup mashed strawberries
½ tsp. vanilla

Mix together and pour over cooled cake.

LEMON POUND CAKE

1 package lemon cake mix
1 package instant lemon pudding
1 package lemon frosting
1/3 cup oil
1 cup water
4 large eggs

Blend all ingredients together on medium for 2 minutes.

Pour into greased or lined cake or Bundt pan.

Bake at 350 degrees for 35 minutes or until a toothpick can be inserted and then removed clean.

Cool completely and frost.

ORANGE JUICE CAKE

Cake:

1 package yellow butter cake mix
1 package instant vanilla pudding
1 cup orange juice
½ cup oil
4 eggs
½ cup of nuts

Grease and flour Bundt pan.
Pour chopped nuts over bottom.
Mix remaining ingredients and pour over nuts.
Bake at 325 degrees for 1 hour or until a toothpick can be inserted and then removed clean.

Glaze:

½ cup orange juice
1 stick butter

Bring to a boil for 2 minutes while stirring.
Pour over hot cake and let set for 30 minutes.

SEVEN-UP CAKE

Cake:

1 lemon supreme cake mix
1 small package instant lemon pudding
4 eggs
¾ cup oil
1 can (10oz) of 7-Up

Mix cake mix, pudding, eggs, oil and 7-Up together. Bake at 325 degrees in a greased or lined pan for 30 minutes or until a toothpick can be inserted and then removed clean.

Icing:

2 tbsp. flour
1 stick butter
1 small can of coconut
1 small can crushed pineapple (drained)
2 eggs
1 ½ cup sugar

Mix and then cook flour, eggs, sugar, butter and pineapple over low heat until thick.
Remove from heat and add coconut. Pour over cake.

CARROT CAKE

Cake:

1 ½ cups oil
2 cups sugar
4 eggs
2 cups flour
2 tsp. baking soda
1 pinch salt
3 cups grated carrots
2 tsp. cinnamon
1 tsp. vanilla

Mix oil and sugar together, blend in eggs until smooth.
Mix in remaining cake ingredients and beat until smooth.
Pour into greased or lined pan and bake at 350 degrees
for 35 minutes.

Icing:

¼ cup melted butter
1 8oz cream cheese
1 lb. powdered sugar

Mix butter and cream cheese together until smooth, then
add sugar gradually.
Beat until smooth and pour over cooled cake.

GERMAN CHOCOLATE CAKE

Cake:

1 4oz package of German Sweet Chocolate
½ cup water
2 cups flour
1 tsp. baking soda
¼ tsp. salt
1 cup (2 sticks) melted butter
2 cups sugar
4 separated eggs
1 tsp. vanilla
1 cup buttermilk

Preheat oven to 350 degrees. Cover the bottoms of 3 9" round cake pans with wax paper and grease the sides.

Microwave chocolate and water in a large bowl on high 1 ½ to 2 minutes or until chocolate is almost melted, stirring after 1 minute. Stir until chocolate is completely melted.

Mix flour, baking soda and salt. Set aside.

Beat butter and sugar in a large bowl on medium until

light and fluffy.

Add egg yolks 1 at a time.

Blend in melted chocolate and vanilla.

Add flour alternately with buttermilk and beat until well blended.

Beat egg whites in a small bowl on high until stiff peaks form. Gently stir into batter. Pour evenly into prepared pans.

Bake for 30 minutes or until a toothpick can be inserted and then removed clean. Cool and remove wax paper.

Filling & Frosting:

¾ cup evaporated milk
½ cup firmly packed light brown sugar
½ cup sugar
½ cup butter
1 tsp. vanilla
3 lightly beaten egg yolks
1 1/3 cup (3oz can) shredded coconut
1 cup chopped pecans

In a saucepan over medium heat combine milk, sugar, butter and vanilla.

Bring to a full boil while stirring constantly.

Remove from heat, mixture may appear a little curdled.

Quickly stir a small amount of hot liquid into the beaten egg yolks, return egg yolk mixture to the hot mixture in the sauce pan and blend well.

Return to a boil and stir constantly.

Remove from heat and stir in coconut and pecans.

Cool to spreading consistency beating occasionally.

SOCK-IT-TO-ME CAKE

Cake:

½ pt. sour cream
4 eggs
1 box butter cake mix
½ cup sugar
2/3 cup oil
1 cup nuts
1 tsp. vanilla

Mix all ingredients together and pour ½ of it in a greased or lined pan.

Take 2 tsp. brown sugar and 1 tsp. cinnamon. Sprinkle over half in pan.

Pour in the rest and bake at 350 degrees for 1 hour.

Glaze:

One cup of powdered sugar and sweet milk. Mix until desired consistency.

APPLE CRISP

4 cups of peeled, sliced apples
1/3 cup melted butter
1 tsp. lemon juice
½ cup flour
1 cup oatmeal
½ cup brown sugar
½ tsp. salt
1 tsp. cinnamon

Place sliced apples in greased shallow pan.

Sprinkle with lemon juice.

Combine dry ingredients and add melted butter. Mix until crumbly.

Sprinkle crumb mixture on top of apples.

Bake at 375 degrees for 30 minutes or until apples are tender.

TURTLE CAKE

1 box German chocolate cake mix
1 14oz. package or caramels
½ cup evaporated milk
½ cup butter
1 cup chocolate chip
1 cup broken pecans

Mix cake mix according to box directions.

Grease a 9 x 13 pan.

Pour ½ of cake mix in pan.
Bake for 15 minutes at 350 degrees.

Melt caramels, milk and butter on low heat.

Pour caramel mixture over hot cake mix.
Bake an additional 25 minutes.

Frost with chocolate icing if desired.

FUDGE PIE

1 ½ cup sugar
¼ cup cocoa
3 eggs
1 melted stick of butter
2 tsp. vanilla

Stir all ingredients together and pour in unbaked pie shell.

Bake at 325 degrees for 30 minutes or until a toothpick can be inserted and then removed clean.

TOASTED COCONUT PIE

3 beaten eggs
½ cup melted butter
2 tsp. lemon juice
1 ½ cup sugar
1 tsp. vanilla
1 1/3 cup coconut

Mix all ingredients together until smooth and bake at 350 degrees for 40 minutes or until a toothpick can be inserted and then removed clean.

CHESS PIE

1 ½ cups sugar
1 tsp. vanilla
3 eggs
1 tsp. vinegar
1/3 cup softened butter
1 tbsp. corn meal
1/3 cup milk

Preheat oven to 350 degrees.
Mix all ingredients together and pour into unbaked pie shell.
Bake 30 to 45 minutes or until a toothpick can be inserted and then removed clean.

PIE CRUST

1 ½ cups all-purpose flour
½ teaspoon salt
½ cup shortening
¼ cup ice water

Combine flour and salt. Cut in shortening until crumbly.
Gradually add water, tossing with a fork until dough
forms.
Divide dough into half.
Roll out one half to fit a 9" pie plate for bottom crust.
Roll out second half to cover pie.

BUTTERMILK PIE

¼ cup flour
½ tsp. vanilla
½ cup melted butter
¾ cup buttermilk
1 ¾ cups sugar
½ tsp. salt
3 beaten eggs

Combine all ingredients and pour into unbaked pie shell.

Bake at 350 degrees for 45 to 50 minutes or until a toothpick can be inserted and then removed clean.

PECAN PIE

1 melted stick of butter
2 eggs
1 tbsp. flour
1 cup pecans
1 cup sugar
¾ cup white syrup
Vanilla to taste (1 to 1 ½ tsp.)

Combine all ingredients and pour into uncooked pie shell.

Bake for 30 minutes at 350 degrees.

Heavenly Manna

CHOCOLATE PECAN PIE

1 cup sugar
1/3 cup cocoa
3 beaten eggs
1 cup pecans
¾ cup light corn syrup
1 tbsp. butter
1 tsp. vanilla

Preheat oven to 350 degrees.

Mix all ingredients together and pour into unbaked pie shell.

Bake until syrup has set, about 1 hour.

FRUIT PIZZA

1 17oz. roll of sugar cookies
1 8oz. package cream cheese
¼ cup sour cream
2 tbsp. sugar
½ tsp. almond extract
lemon juice (coat fruit to keep from browning)
fruit: your favorite fruits & nuts (apples, bananas,
nectarines, strawberries, grapes, almonds, etc.)

Preheat oven to 375 degrees.

Line or spray large round pizza sheet.

Open cookie dough and cut into equal slices. Cover your
pan completely, pressing down to make 1 large cookie.
Cook for 13 to 15 minutes until done. Cool.

Mix cream cheese, sour cream, sugar and almond extract
until smooth. Pour over cooled cookie.

Slice fruits and arrange on cream cheese topping.
Keep refrigerated.

SUGAR COOKIES

1 cup butter
1 cup sugar
1 egg
2 ½ cups flour
½ tsp. baking soda
1 tsp. salt
2 tsp. vinegar
1 tsp. vanilla
1 ½ tsp. lemon juice

Mix all ingredients.

Refrigerate for 10 minutes.

Using a spoon, scoop out small amounts, round into balls and place on greased or lined cookie sheet.

Use a fork and indent the tops of cookies.

Sprinkle with sugar.

Bake at 400 degrees for 10 to 12 minutes, until done.

PEANUT BUTTER COOKIES

¾ cup fat
¾ cup brown sugar
¾ cup white sugar
1 cup peanut butter (creamy or chunky)
2 eggs
2 ½ cups flour
½ tsp. salt

Mix ingredients.

Use spoon to scoop out small amounts and roll into no larger than 1" balls.

Place on greased or lined cookie sheet and flatten across top of each ball with fork.

Bake at 350 degrees for 10 minutes.

COCONUT OATMEAL COOKIES

½ cup butter
1 cup brown sugar
1 egg
1 cup rolled oats
½ tsp. salt
½ cup coconut
1 cup flour
½ tsp. baking powder
½ tsp. baking soda

Mix all ingredients.

Use spoon to scoop out small amounts and roll into no large than 1" balls.

Place on greased or lined cookie sheet.

Bake at 375 degrees for 10 minutes.

BLACK WALNUT CHEWIES

1 stick butter
1 ½ cup. Graham crackers
1 cup black walnuts pieces
1 cup coconut flakes
1 ½ cup chocolate chips
1 cup evaporated milk
½ cup sugar

Melt butter and mix with graham crackers and press into greased or lined baking pan.

Top with chocolate chips, coconut and nuts.

Mix milk and sugar. Pour over top.

Bake at 350 degrees in a 13x9" pan for 25 to 30 minutes or until done.

5 MINUTE FUDGE

1 12oz. bag semi-sweet chocolate chips
¾ bag butterscotch chips
1 14oz. can condensed milk
1 tsp. vanilla

Stir and melt on low heat.

Spoon into non-stick pan.

Refrigerate for 30 minutes before cutting.

PEANUT BUTTER BARS

1 ½ cup sugar
¼ cup brown sugar
1 cup peanut butter (creamy or crunchy)
1 cup flour
4 eggs
¾ tsp. vanilla

Combine all ingredients.

Spread in greased or lined pan.

Bake at 350 degrees for 35 minutes.

CHOCOLATE PEANUT BUTTER BALLS

2 sticks butter
1 cup of crunchy peanut butter
1 cup oats
1 tsp. vanilla
1 box powdered sugar
1 small can of coconut
½ cup raisins (optional)

Combine all ingredients together.

Refrigerate for 10 minutes.

Using a spoon, scoop out small amounts and roll into no bigger than 1" balls.

Melt one bag of semi-sweet chocolate chips and dip balls into chocolate.

Keep refrigerated.

BLUEBERRY BANANA DELIGHT

¾ cup melted butter
1/3 cup flour
1 8oz package cream cheese
1 cup sugar
1 large ripe banana
1 16oz blueberry pie filing
1 large cool whip
1 small bag broken nuts

Mix butter, flour and in greased or lined pan, bake at 275 degrees for 45 minutes.

Mix cream cheese and sugar until smooth. Pour ½ of mixture over cooled crust.

Slice and add layer of bananas.

Repeat. Top with cool whip.

Keep refrigerated.

MONKEY BREAD

3 cans biscuits
1 cup sugar
3 tbsp. cinnamon
1 cup chopped nuts
1 ½ stick butter
1 cup brown sugar

Cut each biscuit into 4 pieces.

Mix cinnamon and sugar.

Roll biscuits in mixture and arranged in greased Bundt pan.

Layer with nuts and raisins and apple bits.

Melt butter and stir in brown sugar.

Pour over arranged biscuits.

Bake at 350 degrees for 30 minutes.

CREAM CHEESE POUND CAKE

3 cups sugar
3 cups flour
3 sticks butter
6 large eggs
Pinch of salt
1 ½ tsp. vanilla

Blend all ingredients together on medium until smooth.

Pour into greased or lined cake pan.

Bake at 325 degrees for 1 hour or until toothpick can be inserted in the middle and removed clean.

CHOCOLATE MOUSSE

1 cup crushed pecans
1 cup crushed vanilla wafers
1 stick melted butter
1 cup powdered sugar
1 cup whip cream
1 8oz. cream cheese
2 family size instant chocolate vanilla pudding (mix following box directions)

Use ¾ cup of pecans and mix with vanilla wafers and butter. Press into bottom of pan.

Mix powdered sugar and cream cheese until smooth. Pour over wafer layer.

Mix chocolate pudding according to box directions and pour over cream cheese layer.

Cover top with whipped cream.

Keep refrigerated.

CHOCOLATE GRAVY

¼ cup cocoa
3 tbsp. flour
¾ cup sugar
2 cups whole milk
1 tbsp. melted butter
2 tsp. vanilla

Sift the cocoa, flour and sugar together in pan.

Pour in milk and mix well.

Cook over medium heat, stirring frequently, until consistency is thicker like gravy.

Remove from heat and stir in melted butter and vanilla.

Serve immediately over hot biscuits.

COCONUT CAKE

Cake:

2 ¼ cups flour
2 tsp. baking powder
½ tsp. salt
3 large coconuts or ½ cup freshly grated coconut
1 ½ cups sugar
10 tbsp. melted butter
3 large eggs

Preheat oven to 350 degrees.

Grease the sides of 2 9" round cake pans. Line bottoms with greased and floured parchment paper.

Puncture the coconut shells with 2 holes using nails. Remove nails and place coconuts upside down on glasses to drain. Break open the shells and remove the coconut meat. Grate.

Sift flour and baking powder into bowl. Add salt and set aside.

In another bowl, mix butter and gradually add the 1 ½ cups of sugar

Add the 3 eggs one at a time and beat well.

Slowly add about 1/3 of the flour with ½ of the milk, coconut and vanilla. Beat on low until well blended.

Repeat with remaining mixture.

Spread the batter into the 2 pans and bake for 30 minutes or until toothpick can be inserted in the middle and removed clean. Cool.

Frosting:

2 large egg whites
1 cup sugar
½ cup water
1 ½ to 2 ½ cups grated coconut

Mix the ½ cup of water and 1 cup of sugar to a boil. Cover and cook without stirring for 1 minute.

Uncover and continue to boil, stirring frequently the mixture is hot enough to spin a thread when a little is dropped from a spoon.

Remove from heat and set aside.

Beat the eggs until fluffy and soft peaks form.

On high, gradually add the sugar syrup in a thin stream.

Beat until fluffy enough to make peaks.

Frost the 1st layer of cake. Cover top of 1st layer with grated coconut.

Add second layer of cake and frost. Cover top and all sides with grated coconut.

Refrigerate.

STRAWBERRY CHEESECAKE BARS

1 pouch of sugar cookie mix
1/3 cup melted butter
2 tbsp. flour
3 eggs
2 8oz. packages of softened cream cheese
¾ cup sugar
1 tsp. vanilla
1 jar strawberry spreadable topping

Preheat oven to 350 degrees.
Grease or line 13x9 pan.

In bowl stir in cookie mix, butter, flour and 1 egg until a soft dough forms.
Press evenly into prepared pan. Bake for 15 to 18 minutes. Cool.
In bowl beat cream cheese, sugar, vanilla and 2 eggs on medium until smooth. Spread over crust.
Place strawberry topping in zipper sandwich bag. Cut one bottom corner off. Squeeze bag, making swirls across entire top of cream cheese mixture.
Bake for 25 to 30 minutes. Keep refrigerated.

CHOCOLATE ORANGE PASTRIES

1 3oz softened cream cheese
3 tsp. grated orange peel
1 refrigerated but softened pie crust
¼ cup Orange Marmalade
½ cup dark chocolate chips
1 beaten egg
2 tsp. sugar

Heat oven to 350 degrees. Line cookie sheet.
Stir cream cheese and orange peel until blended.
Unroll pie crust and spread cream cheese mixture over crust.

Microwave marmalade for 10 seconds.
Brush marmalade evenly over cream cheese mixture.

Cut crust into 16 wedges.
Sprinkle chocolate chips over wedges.

Roll each wedge and place on cookie sheet.
Bake for 12 to 15 minutes until golden brown.

STRAWBERRY CREAM CHEESE DUMPLINGS

2 cups sugar
1/3 cup butter
1 8oz can crescent dinner rolls
½ cup strawberry jam (any other flavor may be substituted)
2 oz. cream cheese
3 tbsp. apple juice

Preheat oven to 350 degrees. Grease or line an 8" pan.

Mix 1 ½ cups of sugar, cream cheese and butter together until smooth.

Spread on slices of crescent rolls.

Spread jam across cream cheese mixture.

Roll up crescent rolls.
Pour apple juice over rolls and coat with remaining sugar.

Bake 18 to 25 minutes or until rolls are golden brown and baked through.

LEMON – CREAM CHEESE CRESCENT DANISH

Danish:

1 8oz crescent dough sheet or 1 8oz crescent dinner rolls

1/3 cup or 8oz cream cheese spread

3 tbsp. powdered sugar

8 tsp. lemon curd

Preheat oven to 375 degrees.

Cut dough into 8 slices. Place 2" apart on a cookie sheet.

Press each slice into 3" rounds, leaving a slight ridge around the edge.

Mix cream cheese and 3 tbsp. of powdered sugar.

Spoon about 2 tsp. of mixture onto the center of each dough round.

Top each with 1 tsp. of lemon curd.

Bake 12 to 14 minutes or until golden brown. Cool 5 minutes.

Glaze:

½ cup of powdered sugar

2 tsp. milk

Mix ½ cup of powdered sugar with milk to desired consistency. Drizzle glaze over Danish. Serve warm.

PUMPKIN ROLL

3 large eggs
2/3 cup canned pumpkin
¾ cup all-purpose flour
½ teaspoon salt
2 teaspoons cinnamon
1 cup confectioner's sugar
½ cup melted butter, cooled

1 cup sugar
1 teaspoon lemon juice
1 teaspoon ground ginger
1 teaspoon baking powder
1 cup chopped pecans
2 3oz. pkgs cream cheese
½ teaspoon vanilla

Preheat oven to 350 degrees. Grease and flour 17 ½" x 12 ½" pan.

Beat eggs, sugar, pumpkins and lemon juice until smooth. Sift together the flour, ginger, salt, baking powder and cinnamon. Add these ingredients to the egg mixture and mix until completely combined. Spread onto the prepared pan. Sprinkle with chopped pecans. Bake until done, about 14 minutes. Let the cake cool in the pan for at least 5 minutes.

Invert the cake onto a wire rack if available. Sprinkle some of the confectioner's sugar on a large tea towel and carefully transfer the cake to the towel, folding the sides of the towel over the cake. Roll the cake up in the towel and cool in the refrigerator thoroughly for 45 minutes.

With a mixer, combine the confectioner's sugar, cream cheese, butter and vanilla and beat until smooth. Carefully unroll the cooled cake and spread the mixture on top of the cake Gently re-roll the cake up and refrigerate it until you're ready to slice and serve.

Dust with confectioner's sugar just before serving.

CHOCOLATE COCA-COLA CAKE

Cake:

2 cups flour
¼ cup cocoa
1 tsp. baking soda
½ tsp. salt
1 ½ cups mini marshmallows
1 cup Coca Cola
½ cup buttermilk
1 cup softened butter
1 ¾ cups sugar
2 beaten eggs
2 tsp. vanilla

Frosting:

½ cup butter
1/3 cup coca cola
3 tbsp. cocoa
4 cups powdered sugar
1 tbsp. vanilla

Preheat oven to 350 degrees. Spray or line a 9 x 13 pan.

Combine coca cola, buttermilk and vanilla. Set aside.

Beat butter, sugar at a low speed until fluffy. Add eggs one at a time and beat until blended.

Combine flour, cocoa, salt and coke. Add to butter mixture alternately with coke mixture. Beginning and ending with flour mixture.

Stir in marshmallows. Pour into pan.

Bake for 30 to 35 minutes. Remove and allow to cool before pouring frosting over cake.

Frosting Directions:

Boil butter, coke and cocoa for 1 minute, stirring constantly.

Whisk in powdered sugar and vanilla until smooth.

Pour over warm cake.

A Good Life Is Created One Sweet Moment At A Time

VANILLA RED VELVET MARBLED POUND CAKE

Cake:

1 cup softened butter
½ cup vegetable shortening
2 ½ cups sugar
6 large eggs
3 cups flour
1 tsp. baking powder
½ tsp. salt
¾ cup whole milk
1 tbsp. vanilla
2 tbsp. unsweetened cocoa
1 tbsp. red food coloring

Glaze:

1 cup sugar
1 ½ tsp. baking soda
½ cup buttermilk
½ cup butter
1 tbsp. light corn syrup
1 tsp. vanilla

2 tbsp. whole milk

Preheat oven to 325 degrees. Grease or line a 10" Bundt pan.

Cream butter and shortening until smooth.

Gradually add in sugar, beating until fluffy.

Add in eggs, one at a time.

Stir together the flour, baking powder and salt.

Add flour alternately with the milk beginning and ending with the flour.

Stir in vanilla.

Transfer half the mixture to another bowl.

To one batch of batter, add cocoa and food coloring. Stir until combined.

Evenly pour half of the vanilla pound cake batter into the prepared pan.

Top that layer with half of the red velvet batter. Smooth the top.

Bake for 60 to 70 minutes or until a tooth pick inserted in

the middle will come out clean. Cool for 20 minutes.

When cooled, add frosting.

Frosting:

On medium heat, bring sugar, baking soda, buttermilk, butter and corn syrup to a low boil. Stir constantly for 4 minutes.

Remove from heat and stir in vanilla. Whisk until smooth.

CROCK POT CHOCOLATE CANDY

Layer each ingredient into the crock pot as listed below.

2 lbs. roasted salted peanuts
1 bar – sweet dark chocolate
12 oz. semi-sweet chocolate chips
2 1/1 lb. bar almond bark

Cook for 3 hours on low. Do not stir.

When done, stir completely and drop about 2 tablespoons in cupcake liners. If necessary, refrigerate to set.

PEANUT BRITTLE

3 cups sugar
½ cup water
1 cup white syrup

Mix and bring to a boil, stirring until it reaches 240 degrees.

At 240 degrees, add:
3 cups peanuts

Continue to cook to 300 degrees and then add:
1 stick of butter.
Once melted, turn off heat.

Mix the following ingredients separately:
1 tablespoon baking soda
1 tablespoon salt
1 tablespoon vanilla

Pour into cooked ingredients until well blended.
Pour on greased baking sheet until cook.
Break into pieces.

GOOEY BUTTER CAKE

1 box yellow cake mix
1 large egg
½ cup melted butter
Mix together and press in a 11" x 13" prepared pan.

Mix:
1 8oz package softened cream cheese
2 large eggs
1 teaspoon vanilla
1 16oz. box confectioner's sugar
½ cup melted butter

Pour over fix mixture.

Bake at 350 degrees until golden brown.

BANANA PUDDING

¾ cup sugar – divided
1/3 cup all-purpose flour
3 separated eggs
45 vanilla wafers – divided
5 ripe, sliced bananas – divided

Dash of Salt
2 cups milk
½ teaspoon vanilla

Mix ½ cup sugar, flour and salt in the top of boiler. Blend in 3 egg yolks and milk. Cook, uncovered, over boiling water, stirring constantly for 10 to 12 minutes or until thickened. Remove from heat, stir in vanilla.

Reserve 10 waters for garnish. Spread small amount of custard on bottom of 1 ½ quart casserole; cover with a layer of wafers and a layer of sliced bananas. Pour about 1/3 of custard over bananas. Continue layering.

Beat egg whites until soft peaks form; gradually add remaining ¼ cup of sugar and beat until stiff but not dry. Spoon on top of pudding, spreading evenly to cover entire surface and sealing well to edges.

Bake at 350 degrees in top half of oven for 15 minutes or until browned. Cool slightly or refrigerate. Garnish with additional wafers and bananas before serving.

GLAZED PRUNE CAKE

Cake:

1 cup cooking oil	1 ½ cups sugar
1 cup buttermilk	3 large eggs
2 cups self-rising flour	1 teaspoon baking soda
1 teaspoon nutmeg	1 teaspoon cinnamon
1 teaspoon vanilla	1 teaspoon salt
1 cup chopped nuts	1 cup cooked prunes

Combine dry ingredients, once mixed add remaining ingredients and mix well.

Pour the batter into a greased/floured 13"x9" prepared baking dish. Bake at 350 degrees for 50 minutes or until done.

Glaze:

1 cup sugar	½ cup buttermilk
½ teaspoon vanilla	½ teaspoon baking soda

Mix all ingredients in a small sauce pan and cook slowly over medium heat until slightly thickened.

Poke holes into the top of the cake when done and pour warm glaze over the top of the cake.

Heavenly Manna

ORANGE CREAM DESSERT SQUARES

1 16.5 oz. roll of refrigerated sugar cookies
2 tablespoons grated orange peel
2 8oz. packages softened cream cheese
¼ cup sugar
½ cup orange marmalade
1 teaspoon orange-flavored liqueur OR
    ¼ teaspoon orange extract
2 eggs
3 tablespoons heavy whipping cream
2 drops of orange food coloring OR
    2 drops of yellow and 1 drop of red food coloring
1 ½ teaspoons melted butter
½ cup white vanilla baking chips

Heat oven to 350 degrees. Press cookie dough evenly on bottom and 1 inch up sides of ungreased 13"x9" prepared baking dish. Sprinkle evenly with orange peel.

In medium bowl, beat cream cheese, sugar, marmalade and liqueur with electric mixer on medium-high speed about 1 minute or until well blended. Add eggs; beat about 2 minutes or until creamy.

Bake about 30 minutes or until crust is golden brown and center is set. Cool for 1 hour.

In small microwave bowl, microwave whipping cream and food color uncovered on high for 30 seconds or just until boiling. Add butter and baking chips; stir until chips are melted. Spread mixture evenly over the bars. Refrigerate about 1 ½ hours or until chilled and firm.

Cut into squares to serve.

CARAMEL CAKE

Cake:

3 cups all-purpose flour
1 teaspoon baking powder
1 teaspoon baking soda
½ teaspoon salt
1 ¼ cup coconut milk

1 ½ cups sugar
4 large eggs
1 cup unsalted butter
1 teaspoon vanilla

Mix all ingredients and bake at 350 degrees until done.

Icing:

In a large bowl place 3 cups confectioner's sugar and set aside.

In a heavy saucepan place ¾ cup butter over medium until melted. Add in 1 ½ cups firmly packed brown sugar. Bring to a simmer and cook for 1 minute, stirring constantly. Remove from heat.

Stir in 5 tablespoons of whole milk and mix with an electric mixer. Add in 1 ½ teaspoons vanilla and ½ teaspoon salt.

Add mixture into bowl of confectioner's sugar and mix well.

Spread over cake.

Made in the USA
Middletown, DE
29 August 2020